GINGER SPICE
IN MY POCKET

GERI

B⊠XTREE

First published in the UK in 1997 by Boxtree,
an imprint of Macmillan Publishers Ltd, 25 Eccleston Place, London,
SW1W 9NF and Basingstoke

Associated companies throughout the world

ISBN 0 7522 1154 4

Photographs: All Action – front & back cover, 1, 3, 13, 14, 17, 18, 21, 28,
31, 32, 33, 34, 39, 40, 43, 44, 48 Capital Pictures – 4, 6, 11, 22, 24 & 25,
27, 38 Retna – endpapers, 9, 36, 47

9 8 7 6 5 4 3 2 1

A CIP catalogue record for this book is available from the
British Library

Design by Blackjacks

Concept by Clare Hulton

Printed in Singapore

GERI SAID
THAT SHE
DIDN'T CRY
WHEN SHE
HAD HER
TATTOOS DONE
BECAUSE
GIRLS ARE
STRONGER
THAN BOYS!

GINGER SPICE CLAIMS TO BE THE BOSSIEST MEMBER OF THE GROUP

GINGER SPICE SAYS THAT YOU CAN'T BEAT ATTITUDE, INTELLIGENCE AND A WONDERBRA: IT'S A LETHAL COMBINATION!

**GERI ONCE
OWNED A
FIAT UNO
WHICH SHE
CRASHED
SEVEN TIMES
IN SIX
MONTHS**

GERI'S IDEAL MAN MUST BE FUNNY AND COOL

MEL B SAYS THAT GERI IS GOOD FOR A CHAT. 'IT'S VERY EASY TO GET INTO CONVERSATION WITH HER... BUT SHE CAN BE TOO OPINIONATED ABOUT THINGS.'

DURING A VIDEO SHOOT GINGER SPICE HAD TO GO TO CASUALTY TO HAVE A FALSE FINGERNAIL REMOVED - FROM INSIDE HER EAR

'MY FAVOURITE WORD IS "EXISTENTIALISM". I CAN'T SAY IT AND I'M NOT QUITE SURE WHAT IT MEANS.'

GERI'S A REAL SOFTY AT HEART — THE FILMS 'DEAD MAN WALKING' AND 'A TIME TO KILL' BOTH MADE HER WEEP

WHEN GERI AND MEL B WERE ON HOLIDAY IN SRI LANKA THEY HANDCUFFED A NIGHT-CLUB OWNER TO A TREE TO PREVENT HIM FROM CLOSING THE CLUB AT MIDNIGHT

GINGER SPICE WANTS BRYAN ADAMS, "COS THE ONLY THING THAT'L LOOK GOOD ON HIM IS ME.' SHE ACTUALLY MET HIM AND SLAPPED HIS BUM. SHE ALSO PINCHED PRINCE CHARLES' BOTTOM WHEN SHE MET HIM

WHEN THE SPICE GIRLS DID THEIR COMIC RELIEF NUMBER GERI WAS SPOOKED BY HOW MUCH JENNIFER SAUNDERS LOOKED LIKE HER

GERI HAS ALSO WORKED AS AN AEROBICS TEACHER, BARMAID AND CLEANER

GERI SPENT
HER EARLY
SHOW BIZ
CAREER IN
SPAIN AS A
NIGHT-CLUB
DANCER AND
SHE EVEN
WORKED AS A
HOSTESS ON A
TURKISH GAME
SHOW

Full name: Geri Estelle Halliwell

Date of birth: 6 August 1972

**Distinguishing marks:
Two tattoos – one is of a
black panther on the base
of her spine**

Height: 5ft 1in

GINGER SPICE HAD A CAKE FIGHT WITH SOMEBODY ON LIVE FRENCH TV!

GERI MADE HER
BROTHER CRY BY
THROWING A STONE
AT HIM. IT HIT HIM IN
THE EYE AND GAVE HIM
A NOSE BLEED

GERI LOVES TO DRESS UP — SHE ONCE TURNED UP FOR WORK WEARING A NIGHTIE

'SOMEBODY STOLE ALL MY RUBBISH! I CAME OUT OF MY HOUSE TO SEE ALL THESE KIDS RUNNING AROUND. THEN I NOTICED THAT MY RUBBISH WAS GONE!'